UNDER OUR MASKS...

A KIDS ACTIVITY BOOK

Coping with masks and social distancing EMOTIONS.

Publication by Wildi One, LLC

Dedicated to the little ones learning something new...you can do it!

Visit Amazon for our potty training kids activity book
Pets Go Potty Too! A Potty Time Activity Book

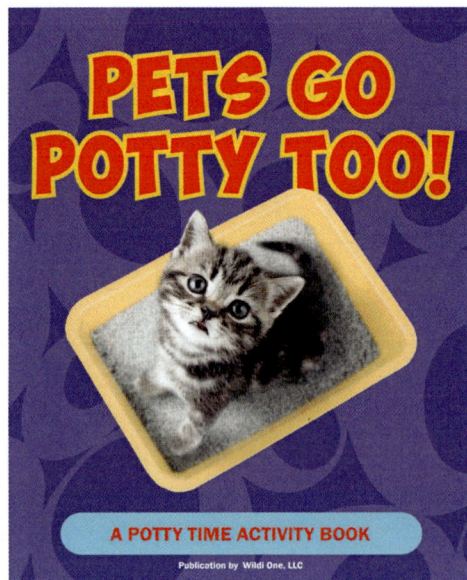

MANY PEOPLE WEAR MASKS AS PART OF THEIR JOBS

FIREFIGHTERS wear masks to breathe while in smoke.

PAINTERS may wear masks to protect themselves from breathing in chemicals.

PILOTS wear masks to breathe oxygen when flying high.

DOCTORS wear masks in surgery to keep their surroundings germ-free.

Under their masks, they can still be themselves and express how they are feeling. Can you think of any other jobs that would be helpful to wear a mask?

SOMETIMES YOU MAY HAVE TO WEAR A MASK TO HELP KEEP GERMS FROM SPREADING.

UNDER YOUR MASK, YOU CAN STILL BE YOURSELF AND EXPRESS HOW YOU ARE FEELING.

CAN YOU USE THE RIDDLES ON THE NEXT FEW PAGES TO FIGURE OUT HOW EACH CHILD IS FEELING UNDER HIS OR HER MASK?

I love to run and **PLAY**. That is something I can do all day.

UNDER MY MASK I WEAR MY...

HAPPY FACE

Wear your mask and look in the mirror. Can you tell if you are SMILING?

FEELINGS FACT

When you smile it means you feel happy. What are some things that make you feel happy?

Something that I do **NOT** enjoy is to stop playing and clean up my toys.

UNDER MY MASK I WEAR MY...

FRUSTRATED FACE

When was a time you felt FRUSTRATED?

What are some positive words you can use next time you feel frustrated?

FEELINGS FACT

Being frustrated means you are not happy that you are not able to do something you want to do. Take a deep breath and try to stay calm. Even when you are wearing a mask, you can still use your words to tell someone how you feel.

When I **DANCE** to a funny song, my crazy moves are never wrong.

UNDER MY MASK I WEAR MY...

SILLY FACE

What is something that makes you feel SILLY?

Can you act silly for five seconds?

FEELINGS FACT

When you feel silly, you probably laugh a lot.

Today I was picked to be first in line. Now it is my time to **SHINE.**

UNDER MY MASK I WEAR MY...

SURPRISED FACE

When was the last time you were

SURPRISED?

What does your surprised face look like?

Think of your favorite place to play. What if you could go **TODAY?**

UNDER MY MASK I WEAR MY...

EXCITED FACE

Can you tell if someone is

EXCITED

by how they move their body? How do you act when you are excited?

FEELINGS FACT

When you feel excited, you have a rush of happy energy.

When someone breaks my favorite toy, it makes my feel like I have lost my **JOY**.

UNDER MY MASK I WEAR MY...

UPSET FACE

Is it easy to tell if someone is **UPSET?**

FEELINGS FACT

When you feel upset, you may feel sad or disappointed that something happened. It is okay to feel upset and talk to someone about it. Practice talking about what upset you today and explain why it made you feel that way.

GREAT JOB guessing the emotions under each mask! You saw kids that felt happy, frustrated, silly, surprised, excited, upset, proud and sad.

Now it is your turn for some games with emotions!

MATCH THE EMOJI WITH THE EMOTION

Draw a line with your finger to match the emoji with the emotion on the face.

SAD   **HAPPY**   **ANGRY**   **SCARED**   **CUNNING**

FOLLOW THE FOX

Trace your finger along the path Mr. Fox takes during his day.

Show me how you look during each of the emotions Mr. Fox experienced today. If you wore a mask, could you still tell what emotion that is?

SOCIAL DISTANCING:

Social distancing is when we have to give more space to people around us even when we wear a mask.

There may be times when we can't play close to our friends. Can you think of other ways to play with your friends while still giving them their space?

Today I earned a good grade on a test. I tried my hardest. I tried my **BEST.**

UNDER MY MASK I WEAR MY...

PROUD FACE

Is there anything you are working hard on? Would you feel **PROUD** if you did well?

FEELINGS FACT

When you feel proud, you are happy with how you performed.

Today I lost my favorite book. I do not know where I should **LOOK.**

UNDER MY MASK I WEAR MY...

SAD FACE

The last time you were **SAD** what made you feel better? What can you do to help someone that feels sad?

FEELINGS FACT

When you feel sad, you feel unhappy. It can be hard to tell if you are sad with a mask on. Make sure you tell someone you are sad and tell them why. "I feel sad because..."

There are also other ways we can **HELP**
keep germs from spreading.

What are some ideas you have?

Turn the page after you thought
of some ideas.

Eventually we will be able to play basketball like this again.

FOR NOW:

stay six feet apart, drink plenty of water, and wash your hands.

If you don't feel well let someone know.
Take some time to play
by yourself until you feel **BETTER.**

Adults may need to check your temperature
and sit you apart from your friends.

FOR NOW:

don't share food or drinks, school supplies,
or any devices you use.

If we can all stay healthy and follow directions, we will no longer have to cover our **EMOTIONS...**